LORD PETER
&
LITTLE KERSTIN

Published in this series:

Lord Peter and Little Kerstin
Warrior Lore
The Faraway North
Scandinavian Ballad Melodies

More by the same author:

The Saga of Didrik of Bern
Stories from Saxo

Original fiction:

The Language of Birds

Lord Peter and Little Kerstin

Mediæval Ballads from Sweden

Ian Cumpstey

Northern Displayers, Skadi Press

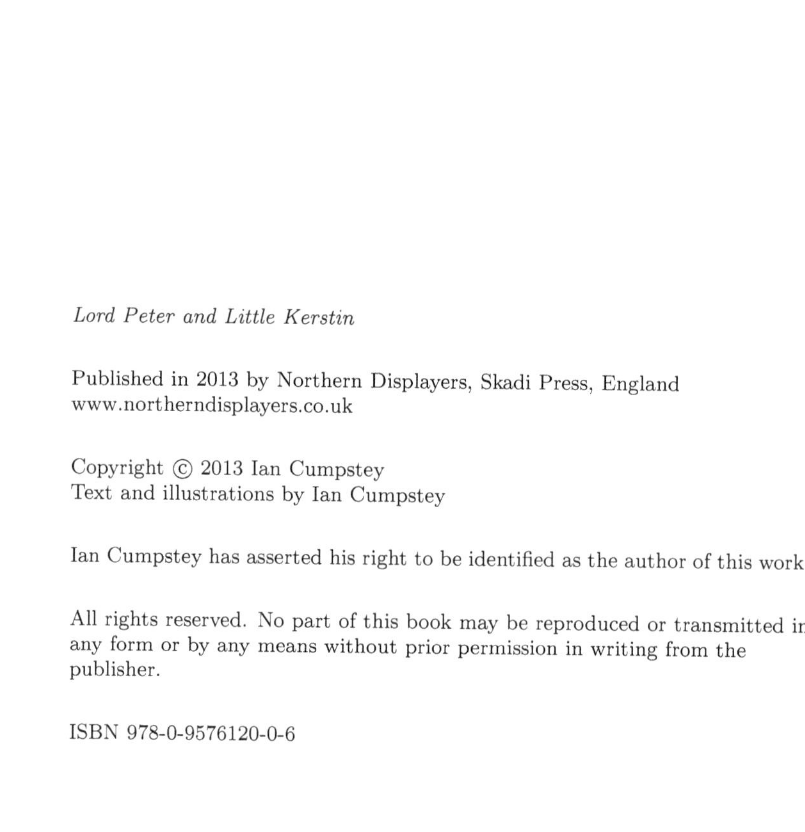

Lord Peter and Little Kerstin

Published in 2013 by Northern Displayers, Skadi Press, England
www.northerndisplayers.co.uk

Text and illustrations by Ian Cumpstey

ISBN 978-0-9576120-0-6

Contents

Preface

A number of Scandinavian folk-ballads from a rich tradition, first sung in the middle ages or in the medieval style, survive in written records. In this book, I present versions in English of ten of the ballads from Sweden. The ballads included here tell tales of love and loss, and feature the supernatural creatures of Scandinavian folklore. The main protagonists of the ballads are often *Sir Peter* and *Little Kerstin*, but it is not the same Sir Peter and little Kerstin who appear in all of the ballads. Sometimes they are lovers, sometimes brother and sister, and sometimes one appears without the other. These names are very common, but there are often versions of the ballads where the protagonists are given different names. In *Sir Olof and the Elves* in this collection, I have let the hero be Sir Olof, which is his name in most versions, although versions are known where he appears as Sir Peter.

As well as the recurrence of these names, many other themes are found as standard in the ballads. For example, a horse is most often a *palfrey grey* (*gångare grå*), the sea is often the *billowy blue* (*böljande blå*), while the *pillows blue* (*bolstrarna blå*) are a preferred resting place. The ballad ending in which three bodies are found in the house is also widespread.

In the ballad *Sir Peter and Little Kerstin*, an example of an apparent reference to another ballad can be seen: Little Kerstin's lack of any difficulty in crossing a bridge and crossing a stream on the way to the wedding is in stark contrast to her predicament (with a similarly gold-shod horse) in *The Power of the Harp*.

The ballads included here fall into one of two forms. The song *Sir Peter's Sea-Voyage* is written in a four-line-per-verse format, with the second and fourth lines rhyming. All of the other ballads included here have a format that is quite common for the medieval Scandinavian ballads. They appear to be written as rhyming couplets. But when they are sung, they are supplemented by additional lines known as the refrain (*omkväde*), which I have included in italics in the first and last verses of each of the ballads. Often one refrain line is sung after the first line and one is sung as the last line of the verse, but other longer or shorter variants are also known. An example of similar usage in the well-known English canon is found in *Scarborough Fair*, where the lines *Parsley, sage, rosemary, and thyme* and *Then she'll be a true love of mine* behave as *omkväde* lines. In the *Scarborough Fair* example, the *parsley* line is apparently completely peripheral to the meaning of the verse, whereas the *true love* line is essential, and in fact it undergoes minor alteration to make sure the sense is followed. The refrains in the Swedish ballads vary from similarly vague natural motifs, such as *Leaves and raspberry-canes* (from a version of *Little Kerstin and the Mountain King*), to themes that reflect the song's story without naturally forming a part of the sentence of the verse proper, such as *They are lying in Brunby* (in *Sir Arvid* — referring to the place where the tragically killed stepsons are buried), or *They're riding so softly with her in the woodlands* (in *Little Kerstin's Enchantment* — as Sir Peter and the very heavily pregnant little Kerstin flee his mother's house), or *She'll come back when the forest grows leaf-green* (in *The Mermaid* — referring to little Kerstin, who was abducted by the mermaid).

Ballads from the folk tradition often exist with many variations. The versions presented here in translation are, in general, collages: I have used one version of each particular ballad as a basis, but may have used verses from different versions of the same ballad, either to replace equivalent verses or to supplement, to create a reconstructed functional and coherent whole.

For some of the ballads, the differences between the versions are minor, while for others, two versions may follow a similar form for most of the story, but have quite different endings. For example, in the version of *Little Kerstin's Enchantment* presented here, the story ends with the making of waxen dolls to fool the mother into believing that her spell has failed; she then inadvertently reveals the means by which the magic can be overcome (*viz* by being in the same place as the chest), and little Kerstin gives birth to her twins normally. But in a different version, after Sir Peter and little Kerstin make the journey away from his house back to her father's yard, little Kerstin eventually gives birth to two twins who are already seven years old (in this case, the curse was that she would remain pregnant for forty weeks and seven years). Little Kerstin dies (understandably), and the newborns wield their swords and swear death upon their grandmother. The ballad *Little Kerstin the Stable-Boy* similarly has numerous possible endings, arising from the different attitudes of the members of the royal family on discovering that little Kerstin is not only a girl, but also that she has had a baby (or twins) by the prince.

References to source materials are given at the end of this book. Sheet music for the ballad melodies (for nine of the ten ballads) is given at the end of this book, and is also available separately.

1 Little Kerstin and Her Man

Little Kerstin she went to ask of her mother:
    Suffer sorrow!
"Is it shameful, to ride to my sick lover?"
    So late in the evening!

"There is no shame, but rather honour,
    "To ride through the land to your sick lover."

Little Kerstin she made her way out to the stall,
    And she looked at the foals, she looked at them all.

She looked at the red, she looked at the bay,
    And she threw the gold saddle on the palfrey grey.

Little Kerstin she rode to Sir Peter's yard,
    And there before her, two small boys stood.

And a small boy went to Sir Peter to say:
    "A maiden has come on her palfrey grey.

"A maiden is standing out in our yard,
    "A beautiful maiden so fair and so good.

"Her bridle's of silver and saddle's of gold,
"But the maiden herself seems so sorrowful."

"Has a maiden come here, so fair and so fine?
"It is little Kerstin, darling of mine.

"Dear mother, you'll make her happy so well,
"For here she has ridden now all by herself."

"I'll make her happy neither badly nor well,
"If you'd have her happy, you'll do it yourself."

Little Kerstin she stepped through the door inside,
Sir Peter he saw her with gentle eyes.

Sir Peter he patted the pillows so blue:
"Come here, little Kerstin, and rest awhile, do!"

"Well I am not weary, and I am not tired,
"But a rest could well be what I desire."

Sir Peter he spoke to his small boys three:
"Fetch in my golden chest to me."

And Sir Peter he gave her a red-gold band:
"There is none like it in all of the land."

Sir Peter he gave her five gold rings:
"And even the Queen doesn't have such things."

Sir Peter he gave her a harp of gold,
And he asked her to play when she grew sorrowful.

Sir Peter he gave her a golden crown red:
"And this you shall wear after I am dead."

"My son, my son, you shouldn't do so,
"But think about your brothers so small."

"My brothers will have their acres and land,
    "Little Kerstin will lose her dearest friend.

"My brothers will have the farm and the yard,
    "Little Kerstin will lose her friend so good."

Sir Peter he lay by the maiden's breast,
    Suffer sorrow!
And there he slept, for ever at rest.
    So late in the evening!

Little Kerstin and Her Man

2 Sir Peter and Little Kerstin

Sir Peter and little Kerstin were sitting together,
The love we wanted to begin
So many glad words they were saying to each other.
All-dearest of mine, I surely will never forget you

Sir Peter to little Kerstin did say:
"On Sunday 'twill be my wedding day."

"If Sunday will be your wedding day,
"Then I would be there to see it, I say."

"My wedding will be too high up in the land,
"For pretty young maidens to come, I'll be bound."

"Your wedding may be so high up in the land,
"But if I am welcome, then come there I can."

"My wedding will be too high up in the hills,
"For pretty young maidens to get there, I feel."

"Your wedding may be so high up in the hills,
"But if I am welcome, then come there I will."

Sir Peter he's having his wedding so soon,
Little Kerstin she's getting her horse new shoes.

Sir Peter he's getting his wedding arranged,
Little Kerstin she's getting her wedding clothes made.

Her clothes they were sewn with pearls and with gold,
Her fingers with precious stones they were full.

Little Kerstin she saddled her palfrey grey,
She rode to Sir Peter's yard away.

Little Kerstin she's riding all over a bridge,
Her horses are wearing red-golden shoes.

Little Kerstin she's riding all over a stream,
The nails of her red-golden horseshoes gleam.

Little Kerstin she rode to Sir Peter's yard,
And there before her, a small boy stood.

The bride she looked out of the window and said:
"Is that a fair maiden out standing in our yard?

"Is there a fair maiden out standing in our yard?
"A fairer maiden I never saw."

More gold had little Kerstin on her fingers so small,
Than Sir Peter had in his golden hall.

More gold had little Kerstin on her dress's hem,
Than Sir Peter had in all of his realm.

Little Kerstin she stepped through the door inside,
Sir Peter he saw her with gentle eyes.

"Welcome, little Kerstin, here to me,
"Now I have mixed for you wine and mead."

"I don't want mead, and I don't want wine,
"But may I sit here by your young bride?"

"You may not sit there by my young bride,
"But go now and fetch for her mead and wine."

Little Kerstin she went and she walked on the floor,
So many tears she shed so sore.

And the bride she asked of the young boys two:
"Who is this maiden who walks on the floor?"

"Sir Peter he had a lover so grand,
"And there is none like her in all of the land."

They were drinking for days, they were drinking for three,
But never the bride her bed she would see.

They were drinking for days, they were drinking for six,
And then to her bed the bride would go quick.

They led the bride to the bridal house,
Little Kerstin she carried the torch and the light.

Little Kerstin she set the bride on a stool,
And she pulled off both her stockings and shoes.

Sir Peter and his bride they lay in the bed,
Little Kerstin she lay the cover over them.

Little Kerstin she stepped out through the door:
"I wish you goodnight, I'll be back no more."

Little Kerstin she ran to the apple grove there,
She hung herself by her light-yellow hair.

And soon the word to Sir Peter arrived:
"Little Kerstin is hung in the apple-tree grove."

Sir Peter out through the door he sprang,
He banged the door so the locks all rang.

"O little Kerstin, how can you hang here?
And while you lived, I held you so dear.

"I'll dig us a grave both deep and wide,
"And there we will lie, both side by side.

"I'll dig us a grave both deep and long,
"And there we two will both belong."

Sir Peter he set his spear to a root,
The point against his heart he put.

Sir Peter he set his spear to a stone,
The point all through his heart was run.

Then in the morning when day grew light,
There were three bodies in Sir Peter's house.

The first was Sir Peter, the second his lover,
The love we wanted to begin
The young bride, who died of sorrow, the other.
All-dearest of mine, I surely will never forget you

3 The Power of the Harp

Sir Peter he plays in the yard with his sword.
    Little Kerstin she weeps in her room at the court.
"All-dearest of mine, Tell me of all of your sorrows!"

"Either you're mourning for saddle or horse,
    "Or for the man to whom you're betrothed."

"No, I'm not mourning for saddle or horse,
    "Nor for the man to whom I'm betrothed."

"Or do you mourn because you are so young,
    "Or do you mourn that the way is too long."

"And I do not mourn because I am too young,
    "Nor do I mourn that the way is so long."

"Or do you mourn that the saddle is tight,
    "Or do you mourn for the golden crown's weight?"

"And I do not mourn that the saddle's too tight,
    "Nor do I mourn for the golden crown's weight.

"But rather I mourn for the river so blue,
  "For there drowned both of my sisters two.

"And rather I mourn for my gold-yellow hair,
  "For soon it will rot in the river down there.

"For it was foretold, when I was new-born,
  "That the Neck would take me on my wedding morn."

"I say then your horse will have new shoes,
  "For a horse will not stumble with red-golden shoes.

"And I say I shall build up a bridge so strong,
  "Although it may cost me five-thousand Marks.

"And I say I shall build up a bridge so broad,
  "Although it may cost me so much more.

"And twelve of my court-men before you shall ride,
  "And twelve more riders on either side."

And they came to the woods with the river behind,
  And there played a hart, and there danced a hind.

And all of the riders rode after the deer,
  And alone they all left little Kerstin to fare.

And when she had ridden up onto the bridge,
  There stumbled her horse with its red-golden shoes.

There stumbled the horse with the gold nails' gleam,
  Little Kerstin fell into the rush of the stream.

Sir Peter he shouted for his young swain:
  "Fetch me my harp! And make haste back again!"

As the first note on the gold harp he strummed,
  The ugly Neck lay in the water and hummed.

As the second note from the gold harp it rang,
The ugly Neck lay in the water and sang.

As the third note on the gold harp he played,
The ugly Neck lay in the water and cried.

Sir Peter he played so beautifully,
That the birds they all danced in the linden tree.

He played so the bark fell away from the birch,
And the weathercock fell from the parish church.

He played so the bark fell away from the beech,
And the hair all fell from the ugly Neck's cheeks.

"Sir Peter, Sir Peter, stop with your tune,
"Your bride fair and pale I will give back to you."

"If ever I get my bride back at all,
"She won't have her nose or her fingers so small!"

"No you'll get her back so pale and so fair,
"As though she were never down in the Neck's lair."

"My bride so young I will take back from you,
"But you'll also give back her sisters two."

And so there was gladness and happiness great,
With daughters and mother together again.

And so there was joy and gladness beside,
And Sir Peter he got back his dearest bride.
"All-dearest of mine, Tell me of all of your sorrows!"

The Neck (*Näcken*) is a water spirit. He lives in streams and waterfalls, and is musically inclined, often playing a fiddle himself. The Neck can lure folk to their death by drowning.

4 Sir Olof and the Elves

Sir Olof he rode out at matins-time,
    And so he came to the mountain high.
The dance it goes on so well in the woodlands

And when he came to the mountain blue,
    An elven-dance came into view.

The elf-daughter reached out her white hand:
    "Come, come, Sir Olof, and dance with me."

"And neither I would and neither I may,
    "For tomorrow will be my wedding day."

The elf-sister reached out her white hand:
    "Come, come, Sir Olof, and dance with me."

"And neither I would and neither I may,
    "For tomorrow will be my wedding day."

The elf-queen reached out her white hand:
    "Come, come, Sir Olof, and dance with me."

"And neither I would and neither I may,
"For tomorrow will be my wedding day."

"Well if you'd not care to dance with me,
"Sorrow and sickness you soon will see."

Sir Olof he pulled his horse around,
But sickness and sorrow he soon had found.

And when he came to his mother's yard,
There before him, his mother stood.

"Welcome home, Sir Olof, to me,
"For you I have mixed both wine and mead."

"I don't want mead, and I don't want wine,
"But rather I want that bed of mine."

His mother then to Sir Olof speaks:
"Why are you pale in your rosy cheeks?"

"I may well be pale in my rosy cheeks,
"For an elven-dance I've had to flee.

"My dearest mother, make my bed,
"And I'll never get up from there again.

"My dearest sister, brush my hair!
"My dearest father, make me a bier!"

"My dearest son, don't speak that way,
"Tomorrow will be your wedding day!"

And the bride sat for days, she waited for three.
But where oh where could her lover be?

And the bride sat for days, she waited for five.
But never she saw her lover alive.

And the bride she saddled her palfrey grey,
And she rode to Sir Olof's yard away.

When she came to Sir Olof's yard,
There before her, her mother-in-law stood.

"Welcome here, O daughter of mine,
"For you I have mixed both mead and wine."

"I don't want mead, and I don't want wine,
"But how is Sir Olof, that dear man of mine?"

"I've not seen Sir Olof since yesterday here,
"He's out in the woods, hunting hart and deer."

"And does he care more for hart and deer,
"Than he cares for his lover dear?

"And does he care more for hart and hind,
"Than he cares for his dearest bride?"

The bride she ran up the high loft's steps,
With stockings of silk and silver-hasp shoes.

She knocked on the door with her fingers so small:
"Get up, Sir Olof, and unlock the door!"

The bride she had fingers so soft and so small,
And so herself she unlocked the door.

The bride laid her head on Sir Olof's breast:
"Sir Olof, Sir Olof, why are you so hushed?"

And the bride she took the silver-blade knife,
And she stuck it right into her own young life.

And when it was day and the day grew light,
So there were three bodies in Sir Olof's house.

The first was Sir Olof, the second his bride,
And the third was his mother, of sorrow she died.
The dance it goes on so well in the woodlands

Alternative two-line refrain from a different version of the ballad (second and fourth lines):
Falling frost and driving dew / Sir Olof will return in the evening

5 Sir Peter's Sea-Voyage

It was the young Sir Peter,
He combed and curled his hair,
And he went to his foster-mother to ask,
How in death he'd fare.

"And you'll not die on a sickbed,
"And you'll not die in war's strife,
"But you should beware of the billowy blue,
"So it'll not shorten your life."

"No I'll not die on a sickbed,
"And I'll not die in war's strife,
"But I will beware of the billowy blue,
"So it'll not shorten my life."

It was the young Sir Peter,
He went down to the strand.
And there he began to build a ship,
All on the snow-white sand.

The ship it was of whale-fish bone,
And the masts they were the same,
And the flags they were of reddest gold,
That fluttered above like flame.

"So today let's have a drink,
"While we can get a beer,
"For tomorrow we shall sail to sea,
"While the wind is blowing clear."

The skipper and the steersman,
Who sailed out from the coast,
Thought not of God the Father,
God's Son, and the Holy Ghost.

They sailed for days they sailed for months,
All on the mysterious sea.
When the wind dropped low, the ship grew slow,
And calm fell silently.

The captain was a wise man,
He wisely spoke his mind:
"Come let us cast the golden dice,
"The biggest sinner to find."

And once the dice on the gameboard's cast,
Between the shipsmen run.
And the lot fell to Sir Peter,
Once to the King's young son.

And twice the dice on the gameboard's cast,
Between the shipsmen run.
And the lot fell to Sir Peter,
Twice to the King's young son.

And thrice the dice on the gameboard's cast,
Between the shipsmen run.
And the lot fell to Sir Peter,
Thrice to the King's young son.

"And as we are so long from land,
"Where never a priest has been,
"So I'll fall down before the masts,
"All to confess my sin."

It was the young Sir Peter,
He fell down on his knees,
And there he did confess his sins,
Before the tall sails-tree.

"Church tables I have plundered,
"And cloisters I have burnt,
"And many are the maidens good,
"Whose honour I have hurt.

"In the forest I have wandered,
"I've murdered and I've robbed,
"And many are the farmer's sons,
"Whose young lives I have stopped.

"If the Lord God he would help me,
"That I could come to land,
"So I would build a church for him,
"All on the snow-white sand.

"If the Lord God he would help me,
"And on the land I'd tread,
"So I would build a church for him,
"And cover its roof with lead.

"If any of you should come to land,
"And my mother asks for me,
"Tell her I serve in a court of the King,
"And I'm doing comfortably.

"If any of you should come to land,
"And my lover asks for me,
"Tell her I'm lost in the billowy blue,
"So she'll not wait for me."

They took the young Sir Peter,
And cast him overboard,
And at last the ship began to move,
Though they were one man short.

6 Little Kerstin the Stable-Boy

Little Kerstin she's cutting out riding clothes,
    Oh dear one!
And away to serve at the court she goes.
    In our stable she served in secret

Little Kerstin she's riding up to the King's yard,
    And the King himself before her stood.

Little Kerstin she spoke to the King so clear:
    "Does the King need a stable-boy this year?"

"A stable-boy I need this year, of course,
    "But I don't have room for your dapple-grey horse."

The young Prince spoke, who was standing by:
    "His horse can be stabled alongside mine."

On the first day she rode out the foals to graze,
    And that night she went with the young Prince to play.

The second day she rode out the foals to the meadow,
    And that night she slept in the young Prince's bed.

The third day she rode out the foals on the farm,
And that night she slept on the young Prince's arm.

"Our stable-boy's grown so wonderfully fat,
"No more can he ride when the sun burns hot.

"Our stable-boy's grown so round and so plump,
"That into the saddle he cannot climb up.

"Our stable-boy's in such a curious mood,
"That he can't pull his riding boot onto his foot."

The young Prince he went to the stable-yard,
To see how little Kerstin the stable-boy fared.

The young Prince he looked in the stable hay,
To see where little Kerstin the stable-boy lay.

The young Prince spread out his cape so blue,
And there bore the stable-boy twin boys, two.

And soon the message came in to the King:
"Little Kerstin she's borne two rosy twins."

And the King he called out over all his court:
"I ask the young Prince right now to come forth."

The young Prince he stepped through the door inside,
And the King he saw him with furious eyes.

"And listen, young Prince, to what I say to you,
"Are you the father of those small boys two?"

And so the young Prince he fell down on his knees:
"Oh my dear father, forgive me, please!"

"So take little Kerstin, you who will be King,
"And make her your wife with these twelve gold rings."

And the ladies and maidens they plaited her hair,
Oh dear one!
For the stable-boy will be a Queen this year.
In our stable she served in secret

7 Little Kerstin's Enchantment

Sir Peter he rode out further on the fen,
    All under the linden so green
He married little Kerstin, a maiden so fine.
    They're riding so softly with her in the woodlands

The very first night that she was a bride,
    Little Kerstin she soon became with child.

Sir Peter he wrapped up his head in a skin,
    And he went to the loft to his mother in.

"Listen, dear mother, and do let us know,
    "How long with child must little Kerstin go?"

"For forty weeks and one year more,
    "So long with child shall little Kerstin go."

"For forty weeks I think is right,
    "So long went Mary with Jesus Christ."

They followed her there, they followed her here,
    They squeezed her so that her death was near.

"As here I can neither live nor die,
"Take me back to the place where you made me your bride."

"But the horses are grazing all out in the meadow,
"And the coachman is lying asleep in his bed."

"If coachman and horses I cannot get,
"I will have to go on my own two feet."

No sooner had these words been said,
Than the horses before the gold carriage were set.

And carefully then, Sir Peter took hold,
And he lifted her into the carriage of gold.

But when they came to the rosy trees,
Her carriage it split into pieces, three.

"A curious woman I must be,
"That my own carriage won't carry me."

Sir Peter the palfrey grey he untied:
"Now I will walk, and you can ride."

"I'm sure all the ladies here will agree,
"To ride would be bad as walking for me.

"I'm sure all the ladies here will attest,
"To sit in the saddle would not be the best."

He gave her his hand and he lifted her up,
And sorely she cried as he carried her forth.

And when they came to the castle gate,
Sir Peter's own sister was standing in wait.

"Are you here, Miss Mette-Lill, sister of mine?
"Can you be a help to this dear wife of mine?"

Miss Mette-Lill she was a maiden so fine,
    She was a good friend to her brother's bride.

And so she made two wax-children small.
    And she wrapped them around in a white-linen shawl.

Miss Mette-Lill wrapped up her head in a skin,
    And she went to the loft to her mother in.

"O mother dear, let your anger be calm,
    "And take your grandchildren into your arms."

"O Lord take pity on me, poor wife,
    "Can I not end this woman's life?

"When I was in the days of my prime,
    "Then I could end a woman's life.

"And I could go down to the strand,
    "And wind a rope from only sand.

"And with my rope I'd tie them so,
    "That twixt the Sun and the Moon you'd go.

"I thought that with my magic ring,
    "I could spell-bind everything.

"I thought I'd spell-bound all the land,
    "Except for the place where my old chest stands."

They fetched up the chest from its place so fast,
    And they set little Kerstin upon it at last.

Sir Peter he spread out his silken cape blue,
    And there little Kerstin bore gentle sons, two.

And his mother was filled with fury so dread,
  All under the linden so green
And soon of her anger his mother was dead.
  They're riding so softly with her in the woodlands

8 The Mermaid

Sir Peter he stood in his mother's hall:
    Blows cold, cold, weather from the sea
"Did I not have a sister so small?"
    Blows cold, cold, weather from the sea

"A sister you had, so pale and so fair,
    "But the mermaid has taken her down to her lair."

Sir Peter he went to stand in the stall,
    And he looked at the foals, he looked at them all.

He looked at the white, and he looked at the brown,
    And the grey he laid his saddle upon.

Sir Peter he rode to the green sea strand,
    All so he could find where the mermaid swam.

"Good day, O mermaid, so fine and so fair,
    "A fairer maiden I never saw."

"If you've not seen a fairer maiden than I,
    "Well I have a handmaid as fair as the day."

"And I will give you my palfrey grey,
"If I could see this handmaid today."

"Well you can keep your palfrey grey,
"Of course you can see my handmaid today!

"If you will ride on home to my yard,
"Where the gates and the locks are of iron so hard."

The mermaid she skipped up the high-loft's stairs,
And all of her handmaids after her stared.

The mermaid she patted the pillows so blue:
"And now, little handmaid, get out of bed, do!

"I'm waking you neither to cut nor to sew,
"But to see a young man who is waiting below.

"There is a young knight in our yard down below,
"And to see him today must my handmaid go."

"How then before a knight can I appear?
"I've not seen the sun now for fifteen round years!"

So the handmaid was set on a red-golden chair,
And she shone like the sun as they dressed her there.

They dressed her up in a silk-sewn shirt,
Where fifteen princesses had sewn their work.

They dressed her up in a dress so blue,
With red-golden thread in the hems so low.

And the mermaid she came and she plaited her hair,
And she set on her head a golden crown rare.

And the handmaid she walked down the high-loft's stair,
And fifteen gold baubles she drew after her.

And the handmaid she walked on the green sea strand,
With a silver cup in her snow-white hand.

"I'll not take the cup from out of your hand,
"Till you tell me the name of your father's land.

"Who is your father, and who is your mother,
"Who are you yourself, and who is your brother?"

"My father is King over so many lands,
"And my mother she is a Queen so grand.

"Sir Peter is my brother's name,
"And I am little Kerstin, I say."

"And if you are little Kerstin, you say,
"Then you are my sister, in Jesus' name."

"And I will give you my five rings of gold,
"If I could borrow your handmaid bold."

"And you can keep your five rings of gold,
"Of course you can borrow my handmaid bold.

"Of course you can borrow my handmaid so fine,
"But before three moons she must be here again."

And then Sir Peter he lifted his hat,
And he bid the mermaid farewell and good-night.

Sir Peter he took her on his palfrey grey,
And they rode to their father's yard away.

And when they came to their father's yard,
There before them, their father stood.

"Welcome home, little Kerstin, to me,
"It gladdens my heart that you're back here with me."

The mermaid she waited for full-moons three,
    But never she got her handmaid to see.

The mermaid she waited for full-moons five,
    But never did her handmaid arrive.

The mermaid she swam in the billowy blue,
    But without her handmaid she had to make do.

The mermaid she waited with a furious face,
    But she had to go back to her hiding place.

"If I had known then how false you had spoken,
    Blows cold, cold, weather from the sea
"Your thieving neck I would have broken."
    Blows cold, cold, weather from the sea

Alternative fourth line refrain from a different version of the ballad (second line refrain is the same as above):
She'll come back when the forest grows leaf-green

9 Sir Arvid

Miss Inga-Lill she was as fair as a rose,
    They are lying in Brunby
And Sir David to her, he did propose.
    So sorrowfully cries Miss Inga

"My sons they are still so small and so young,
    "To give them a stepfather now would be wrong."

Sir David he swore, by all the earth bears,
    That as a stepfather, he would be fair.

Miss Inga-Lill wrapped up her head in a skin,
    She went up to her sons to the high loft in:

"Now listen up, my sons so small,
    "Might I bring a stepfather for you to the hall?"

The eldest son he answered her so:
    "You mustn't get us a stepfather, no!"

The youngest son he answered him thus:
    "You let our dear mother do as she must!"

Before Sir David would ride from the yard,
Miss Inga-Lill had to give him her word.

They'd not been together for months, for three,
And her sons he would neither hear nor see.

Sir David he wrapped up his head in a skin,
And he went to the hall to Miss Inga-Lill in:

"Listen, Miss Inga, to what I have to say!
"It's time your sons rode to the court away."

"My sons they are still so young and so small,
"And the armour is heavy there in the King's hall."

"So they'll not serve in the court, I see,
"But then richest tradesmen they shall be."

And Sir David he built a long-boat new,
So he could betray his stepsons two.

The sail it was of silk so light,
Some pieces in gold, some pieces in white.

It was gilded all from the bow to the stern,
And loaded with mead and with coal to burn.

Miss Inga-Lill went to the strand with her sons,
And there on their feet, their golden shoes shone.

Miss Inga-Lill went with her sons to the strand,
With five gold rings on each of their hands.

Sir David he sent out the boat from the land,
Miss Inga-Lill wept all upon the white sand.

The skipper he was a faithless man,
And he carried out Sir David's plan.

The cup was warm, and the mead was sweet,
And the brothers soon fell fast asleep.

And when Sir Arvid awoke, he saw,
That his brother lay in the flames' red glow.

Sir Arvid he called out to God and to man:
"Let me return to my mother's hand!"

Sir Arvid made a cross on the billowy blue,
And took hold of a stone on the sea-bottom low.

And in came the weather and westerly wind,
And back to the coast was his body blown in.

Sir David was walking down on the strand,
There he found Sir Arvid washed up onto land.

He took the five gold rings from his hand,
And cast him away again out from the land.

And the waves they carried him all away,
Till at last on another strand he lay.

Miss Inga and Sir David were sitting together,
So many glad words they spoke to each other.

But there she could see on Sir David's hand,
The rings he had taken down on the sand.

"The last time those gold rings I saw,
"Those rings my son, Sir Arvid, wore."

"Listen, Miss Inga, don't say such things!
"So very alike are all gold rings."

Miss Inga-Lill waited for months, for three,
But she didn't get her sons to see.

Miss Inga-Lill waited for months, for five,
    But her sons they never came back alive.

Miss Inga-Lill went with her handmaids two,
    And they walked on down to the billowy blue.

And when Miss Inga came down to the strand,
    She found Sir Arvid who had drifted to land.

Miss Inga-Lill walked both up and down,
    So sorely the tears on her pale cheeks ran.

Miss Inga-Lill put on her silken shirt,
    So sorely then did her poor heart hurt.

Miss Inga-Lill took her knife up to bed,
    And she stabbed Sir David until he was dead.

"Those poor little children didn't do any harm,
    "You resented me taking them into my arms.

"God bless the widow with children so small,
    "Who for such a wicked stepfather should fall."

Miss Inga-Lill fetched the burial shroud,
    And she dressed Sir Arvid where he'd been found.

Miss Inga-Lill rode to the church so fast,
    To carry her son to be buried at last.

But when they had come up under the lee,
    They set down the body by the linden tree.

But when they were rested and tried to move on,
    They couldn't lift the body again.

They couldn't have lifted the body again.
    Had they been five times as many men.

"Here over Sir Arvid a church I'll begin,
　　"To sing high mass and matins-song in.

"I pray to God in the kingdom of heaven,
　　They are lying in Brunby
"That once again we may all be together."
　　So sorrowfully cries Miss Inga

This song is associated with a folk tale from near the Kullen peninsula in Skåne in the South of Sweden. The villages of Arild (Arildsläge) and Torekov are named after the two sons, Arild (Arvid) and Tore, reflecting the places their bodies drifted to land. The chapel in the song is at Arild, and is dedicated to St Arild, and the rock that Sir Arvid held onto out at sea, and that was washed into shore with him can also be seen (Arild's rock). This rock is imprinted with the shape of a human figure. Brunby is the name of the local parish district, which explains the *omkväde* line *They are lying in Brunby*.

10 Little Kerstin and the Mountain King

Little Kerstin was riding to matins one day,
    Time is long for me
Out on the road where the high mountains lay,
    But I know a sorrow so deep

And all that she rode and all that she stood,
    The nearer she came to the high mountains blue.

And when she came to the high mountains blue,
    The Mountain King before her he stood.

"Oh listen, little Kerstin, don't rush away.
    "Will you come home to the rocks with me?"

And they rode three times the mountain around,
    The mountain-door opened, and they went underground.

She stayed in the mountain for eight round years,
    She bore seven sons, and a daughter so dear.

Little Kerstin she went to the Mountain King to stand:
    "Oh let me go home to my mother's land."

"Of course you may go to your mother's hall,
"But you mustn't mention your children so small."

And when she came to her dear mother's yard,
There before her, her own mother stood.

"And where have you been for such a long while?
"You've been I suppose in the rosy hills."

"And I have not been in the rosy hills,
"In the mountain I've been for such a long while."

"What's that for a scarf that you have on your hair?
"Like the ones that old women and mothers wear."

"Well I can wear a scarf on my head,
"For now to the Mountain King I'm wed.

"In the mountain I've been for eight long years,
"There I bore seven sons and a daughter so dear."

The Mountain King stepped through the door inside:
"Why are you speaking so badly of me?"

"But I have not spoken so badly of you,
"But only of the good things that you've done for me."

The Mountain King struck her lily-cheek pale,
"Be off to the mountain to your children so small.

"Be off to the mountain and don't you stall,
"And you'll nevermore come to your mother's hall."

The Mountain King took little Kerstin's hand,
And he led her away from her mother's land.

And so off they rode through the murk-woods long,
Little Kerstin she cried, but the Mountain King sang.

They rode three times the mountain around,
The mountain-door opened, and they went underground.

Little Kerstin she sat on the red-golden chair,
And she was so sorrowful in her despair.

The Mountain King gave her a golden horn red,
And now you shall drink both wine and mead.

The first of the drink from the horn that she drank,
She forgot the heavens, she forgot the earth.

The second of the drink from the horn that she drank,
She forgot the sun, she forgot the moon.

The third of the drink from the horn that she drank,
She forgot her father, she forgot her mother.

"In the mountain I was born, in the mountain I'll abide,
Time is long for me
"In the mountain I will live as the Mountain King's bride."
But I know a sorrow so deep

Notes

I have primarily used the ballads transcribed in *Svenska Fornsånger*, 1834–1842, A. I. Arwidsson (*A*) and *Svenska Folkvisor Från Forntiden*, 1814–1816, E. G. Geijer and A. A. Afzelius (*GA*) as the starting point for the English versions presented here. Occasionally, I have supplemented this with sources from elsewhere in the Scandinavian tradition, *Danmarks Gamle Folkeviser*, 1853–1904, S. Grundtvig (*G*), and the online *Ballad Archive of the Norwegian Dokumentasjonsprosjektet* (*N*).

The reference numbers of the ballads under the Types of Scandinavian Medieval Ballad (TSB) and Svenska Medeltida Ballader (SMB) classification systems are also given below.

1 – Little Kerstin and Her Man. From *Liten Kerstin och Hennes Fästeman* (*A*75). (TSB D284 / SMB 136)

2 – Lord Peter and Little Kerstin. From *Herr Peder och Liten Kerstin* (*GA*9), also *Herr Peders Slegfred* (*G*210). (TSB D245 / SMB 122)

3 – The Power of the Harp. From *Harpans Kraft* (*A*149 and *GA*91). (TSB A50 / SMB 22)

4 – Sir Olof and the Elves. From *Herr Olof och Elfvorna* (*A*148),

Herr Olof i Elfvornas Dans (*GA*93), and *Elf-Qvinnan och Herr Olof* (*GA*94). (TSB A63 / SMB 29)

5 – Lord Peter's Sea-Voyage. From *Herr Peders Sjöresa* (*GA*36 and *A*67). (TSB D361 / SMB 164)

6 – Little Kerstin the Stable-Boy. From *Liten Kerstin Stalldräng* (*GA*33 and *A*109). (TSB D396 / SMB 178)

7 – Little Kerstin's Enchantment. From *Liten Kerstins Förtrollning* (*A*134), and also *Hustru og Mands Moder* (*G*84). (TSB A40 / SMB 14)

8 – The Mermaid. From *Hafsfrun* (*A*150 and *GA*92). (TSB A51 / SMB 23)

9 – Sir Arvid. From *Herr Arvid* (*A*167), and also *Herr David og hans Stesønner* (*G*337). (TSB B18 / SMB 45)

10 – Little Kerstin and the Mountain King. From *Den Bergtagna* (*GA*1), *Bergkonungen* (*GA*35), and *Jungfrun och Bergakonungen* (*A*142), and also *Liti Kjersti og Bergekongen* (*N*). (TSB A54 / SMB 24)

Melodies

For those wanting to sing the ballads in English translation, musical notation is provided here for traditional melodies.

Melodies are not always known for the surviving ballad texts. This is because when the ballad collectors were writing down the ballads they heard from singers, they often did not write down the melody. Thus, for one of the ten ballads in this collection, *Sir Arvid*, no melody is included here.

For many ballads, more than one traditional melody is known. Often a ballad was sung in different ways in different places. I have included alternative melodies for several of the ballads here. But this section is certainly not intended to be a comprehensive survey of all the known melodies for these ballads. It is meant to be a useful resource for singers.

Altogether, this book includes 21 melodies for 9 ballads.

Some brief advice for singers follows. Sing in a key that suits your voice. You may have to transpose into a different key to fit your vocal range. If you are hoping that musicians might play with you, choose a key that suits them as well.

When singing these ballads, it will be necessary to fit the words to the melody. Sometimes this may involve singing syllables over more than one note as written (classically: melismatic approach), or rather less often by singing two syllables to a single note as written. A good way to do this is to make sure the stresses in the text fall in the same place in the music for every verse. Within the same ballad, some verses may require a lead-in note (classically: anacrusis), and other verses not. For most of the melodies here, the notation does include such a lead-in note. Of course where the written melody does not include a lead-in note, and it transpires that one is required for a particular verse, the singer must add one.

Enjoy singing!

1 – Little Kerstin and Her Man (i)

from Östergötland

1 – Little Kerstin and Her Man (ii)

from Östergötland

2 – Sir Peter and Little Kerstin

from Norrland

3 – The Power of the Harp (i)

from Sweden

3 – The Power of the Harp (ii)

from Sweden

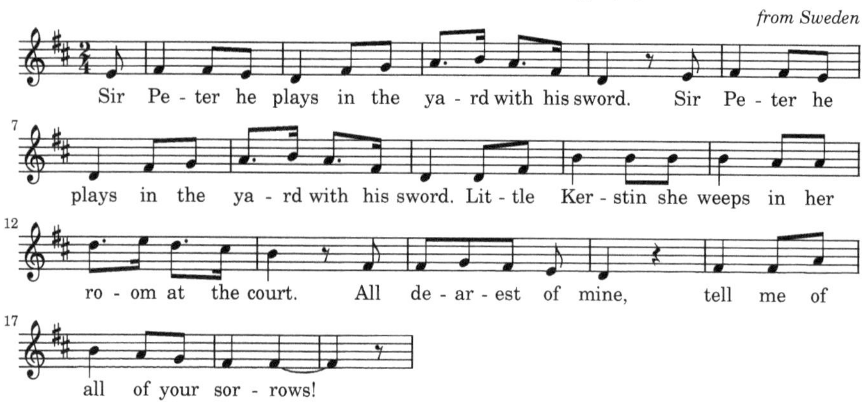

3 – The Power of the Harp (iii)

from Östergötland

3 – The Power of the Harp (iv)

from Västergötland and Värmland

4 – Sir Olof and the Elves (i)

from Östergötland

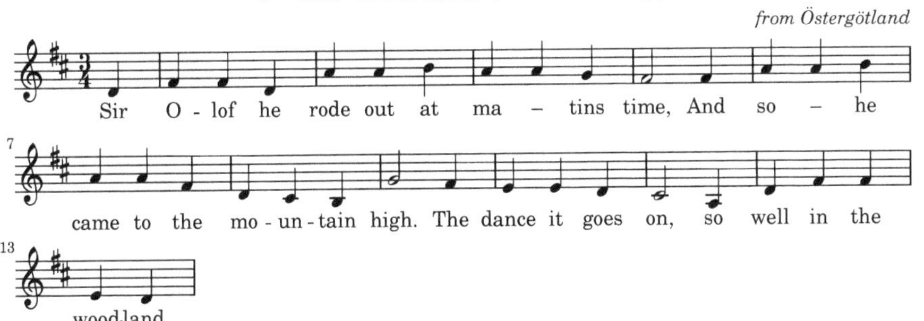

4 – Sir Olof and the Elves (ii)

from Uppland

4 – Sir Olof and the Elves (iii)

from Denmark

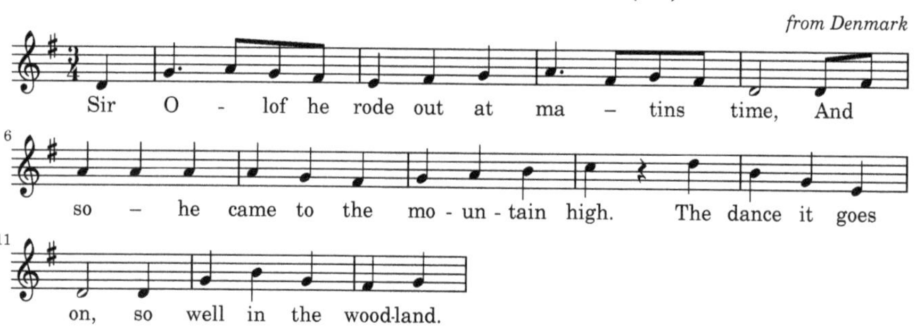

5 – Sir Peter's Sea Voyage (i)

from Östergötland

5 – Sir Peter's Sea Voyage (ii)

from Värmland

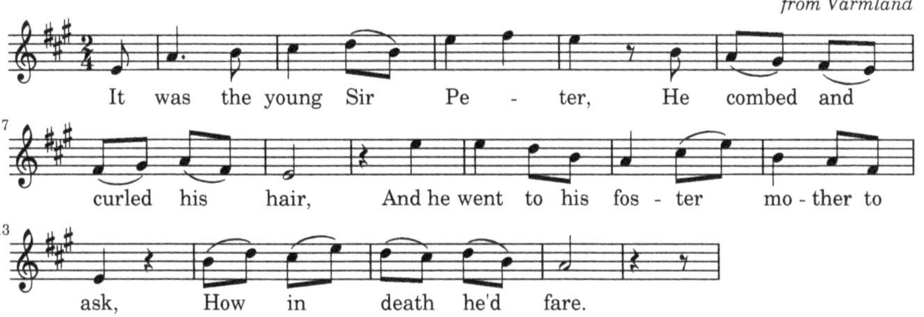

6 – Little Kerstin the Stable Boy (i)

from Västergötland

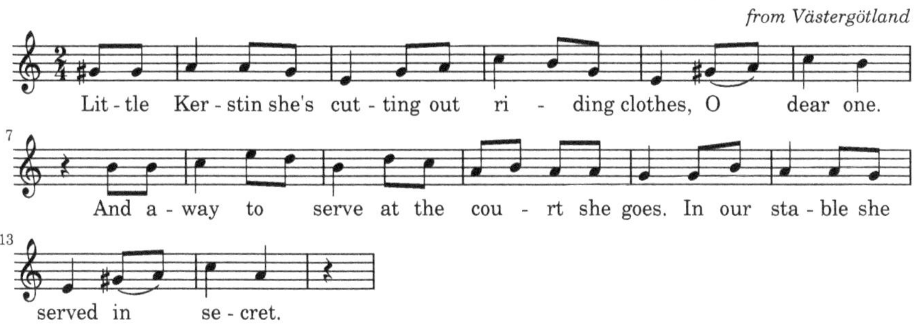

6 – Little Kerstin the Stable Boy (ii)

from Södermanland

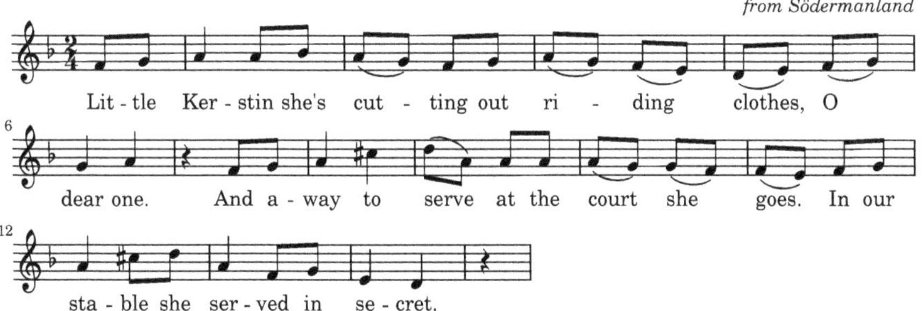

6 – Little Kerstin the Stable Boy (iii)

from Värmland

7 – Little Kerstin's Enchantment (i)

from Östergötland

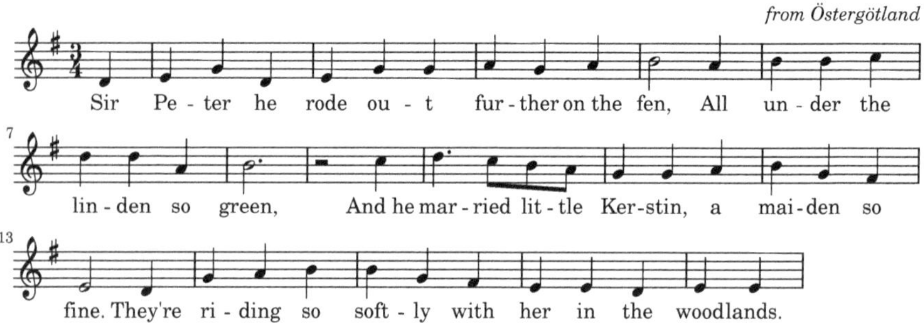

7 – Little Kerstin's Enchantment (ii)

from Östergötland

8 – The Mermaid (i)

from Sweden

8 – The Mermaid (ii)

8 – The Mermaid (iii)

10 – Little Kerstin and the Mountain King

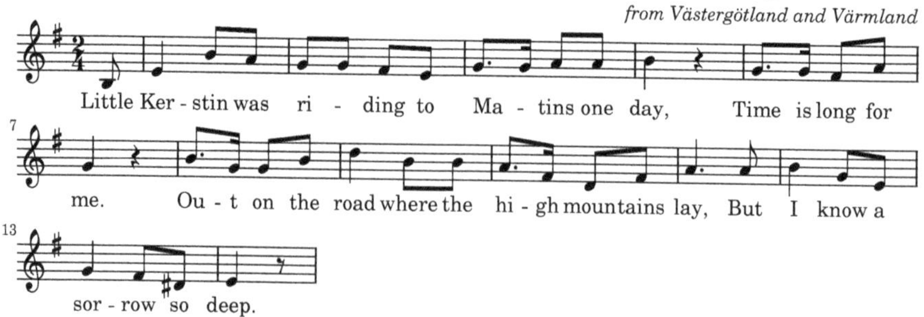

Sources for the melodies are as follows:

1 – Little Kerstin and Her Man

(i) Arwidsson 75C, *Liten Kerstin och Hennes Fästeman.*
(ii) Arwidsson 75B, *Liten Kerstin och Hennes Fästeman*; Ahlström 271, *Liten Kerstin och Hennes Fästeman.*

2 – Sir Peter and Little Kerstin

Ahlström 101, *Herr Peder och Liten Kerstin*; Berggreen (S) 16, *Herr Peder och Liten Kerstin.*

3 – The Power of the Harp

(i) Arwidsson 149B, *Harpans Kraft*; Ahlström 137, *Harpans Kraft.*
(ii) Arwidsson 149A, *Harpans Kraft*; Ahlström 136, *Harpans Kraft*; Berggreen (S) 5a, *Harpans Kraft.*
(iii) Ahlström 138, *Harpans Kraft.*
(iv) Ahlström 140, *Harpans Kraft*; Berggreen (S) 5b, *Harpans Kraft.*

4 – Sir Olof and the Elves

(i) Ahlström 129, *Elfqvinnan och Herr Olof.*
(ii) Ahlström 133, *Herr Olof i Elfvornas Dans.*
(iii) Berggreen (D) 20a, *Elveskud.*

5 – Sir Peter's Sea Voyage

(i) Berggreen (S) 36, *Herr Peders Sjöresa*; Arwidsson 67, *Herr Peders Sjöresa*; Ahlström 194b, *Herr Peders Sjöresa.*
(ii) Ahlström 193, *Herr Peders Sjöresa.*

6 – Little Kerstin the Stable Boy

(i) Ahlström 187, *Liten Kerstin Stalldräng.*
(ii) Bidrag till Södermanlands äldre Kulturhistoria, Södermanlands Fornminnesförening, Vol 1, 1877, No. 4, *Liten Kerstin Stalledräng.*
(iii) Ahlström 190, *Stolts Botelid Stalldräng.*

7 – Little Kerstin's Enchantment
(i) Arwidsson 134B, *Liten Kerstins Förtrollning.*
(ii) Arwidsson 134A, *Liten Kerstins Förtrollning.*

8 – The Mermaid
(i) Arwidsson 150A, *Hafsfrun.*
(ii) Arwidsson 150B, *Hafsfrun*; Ahlström 290, *Hafsfrun.*
(iii) Berggreen (S) 3, *Hafsfrun*; Ahlström 47, *Hafsfrun.*

10 – Little Kerstin and the Mountain King
Berggreen (S) 1, *Den Bergtagna*; Ahlström 26, *Den Bergtagna.*

Arwidsson: A. I. Arwidsson, *Svenska Fornsånger*, Stockholm, 1887.
Ahlström: J. N. Ahlström, *300 Nordiska Folkvisor*, Stockholm, 1878.
Berggreen (D): A. P. Berggreen, *Folke-Sange og Melodier*, Copenhagen, 1855.
Berggreen (S): A. P. Berggreen, *Svenske Folke-Sange og Melodier*, Copenhagen, 1861.
Berggreen (N): A. P. Berggreen, *Norske Folke-Sange og Melodier*, Copenhagen, 1861.
Geijer and Afzelius: E. G. Geijer, A. A. Afzelius, *Svenska folkvisor*, Stockholm, 1880.
Landstad: M. B. Landstad, *Norske Folkeviser*, Christiania, 1853.

www.ingramcontent.com/pod-product-compliance
Ingram Content Group UK Ltd.
Pitfield, Milton Keynes, MK11 3LW, UK
UKHW020418250726
13967UKWH00007B/2703